Adventure Book For Teens:
Cool Things To Do For Teens

Join a regatta.

Drive into
ski fields.

Form a pyramid
in the pool.

Go hiking with
your friends.

Try
skateboarding.

Do exercises with
your friends.

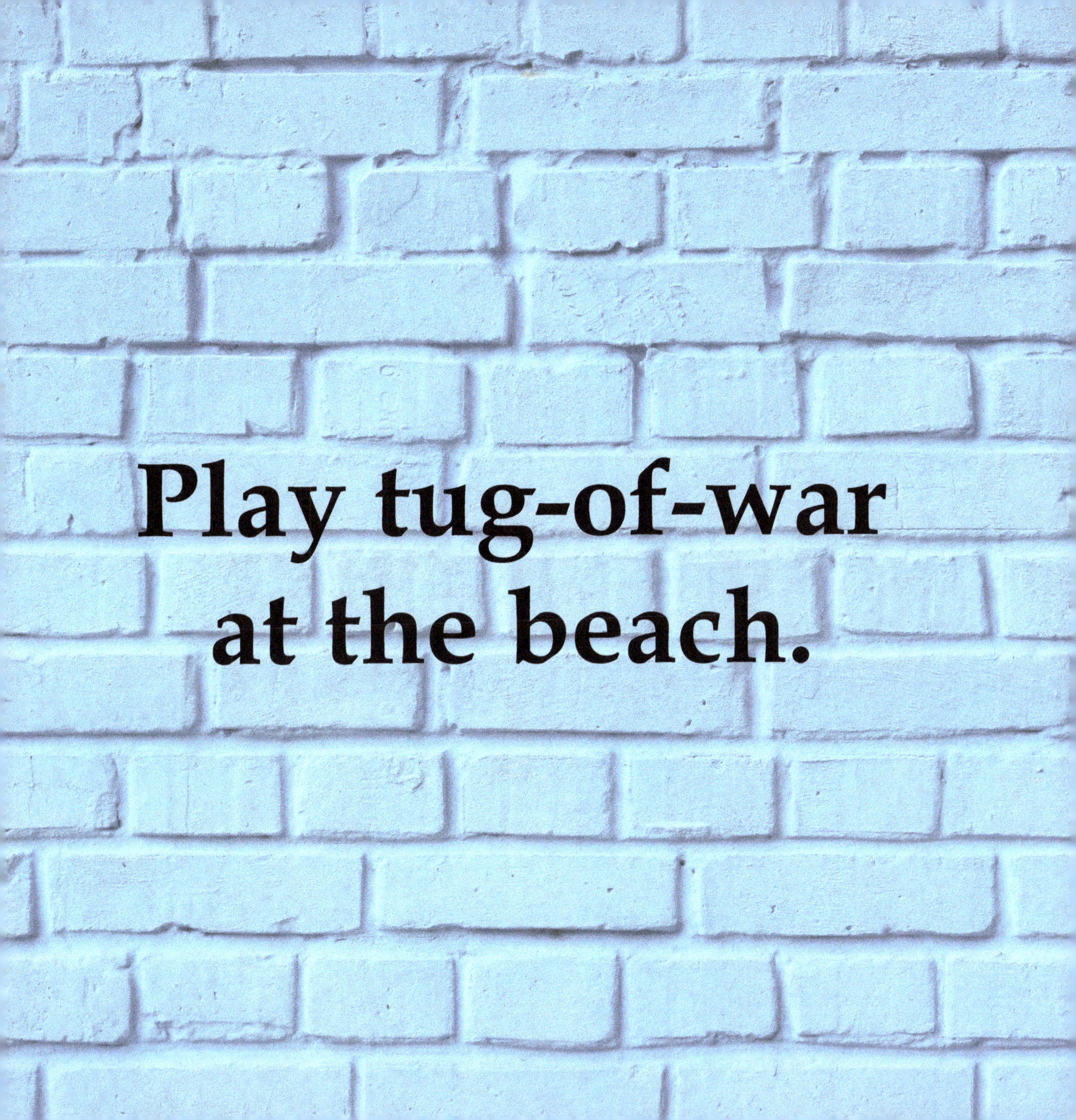

Play tug-of-war
at the beach.

Go surfing.

Kayaking with
friends.

Go mountain
biking.

Jump off a
lake through a
hanging rope.

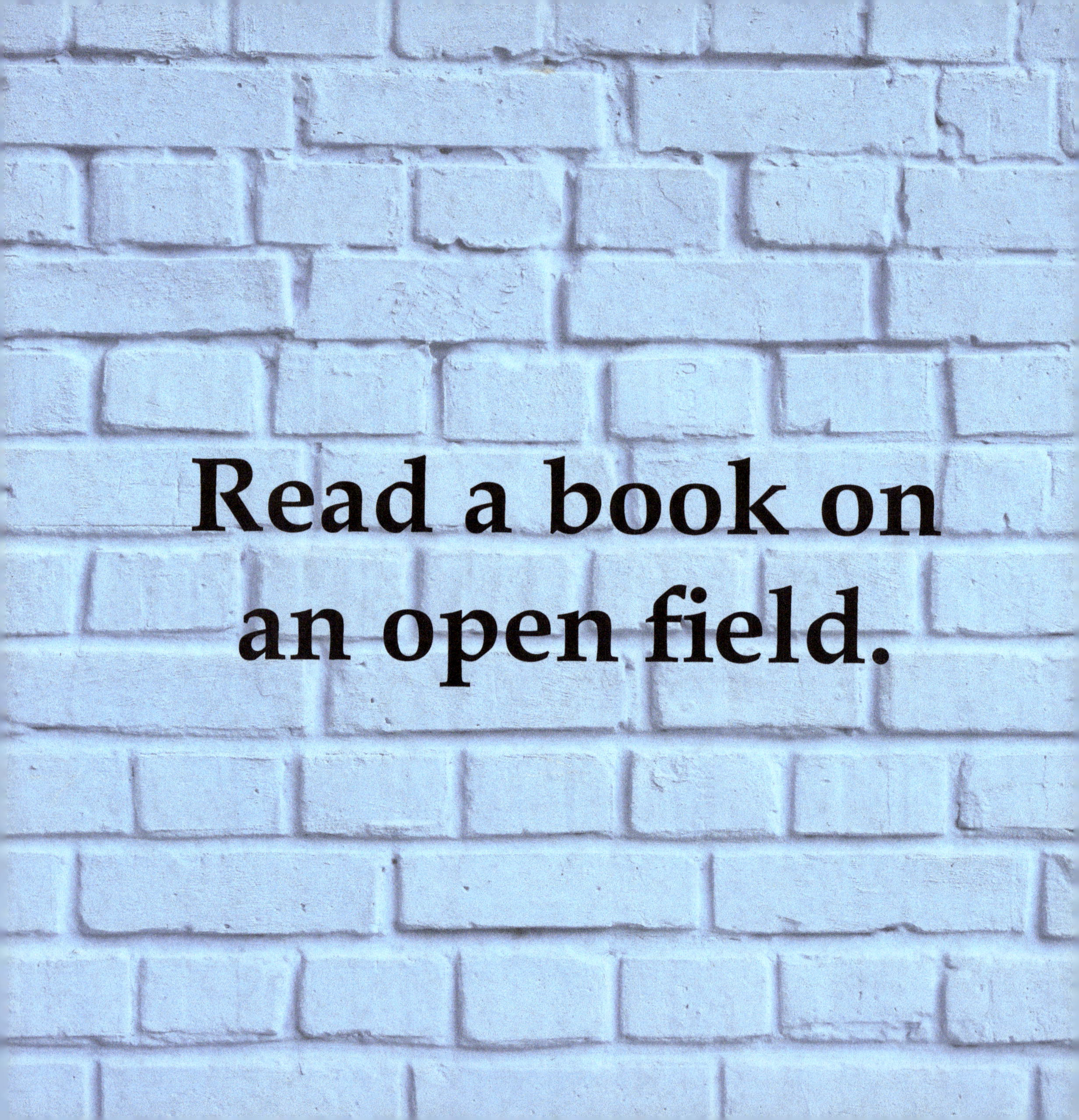

Read a book on
an open field.

Try archery.

Do cartwheel.

Play golf.

Go camping
with friends.

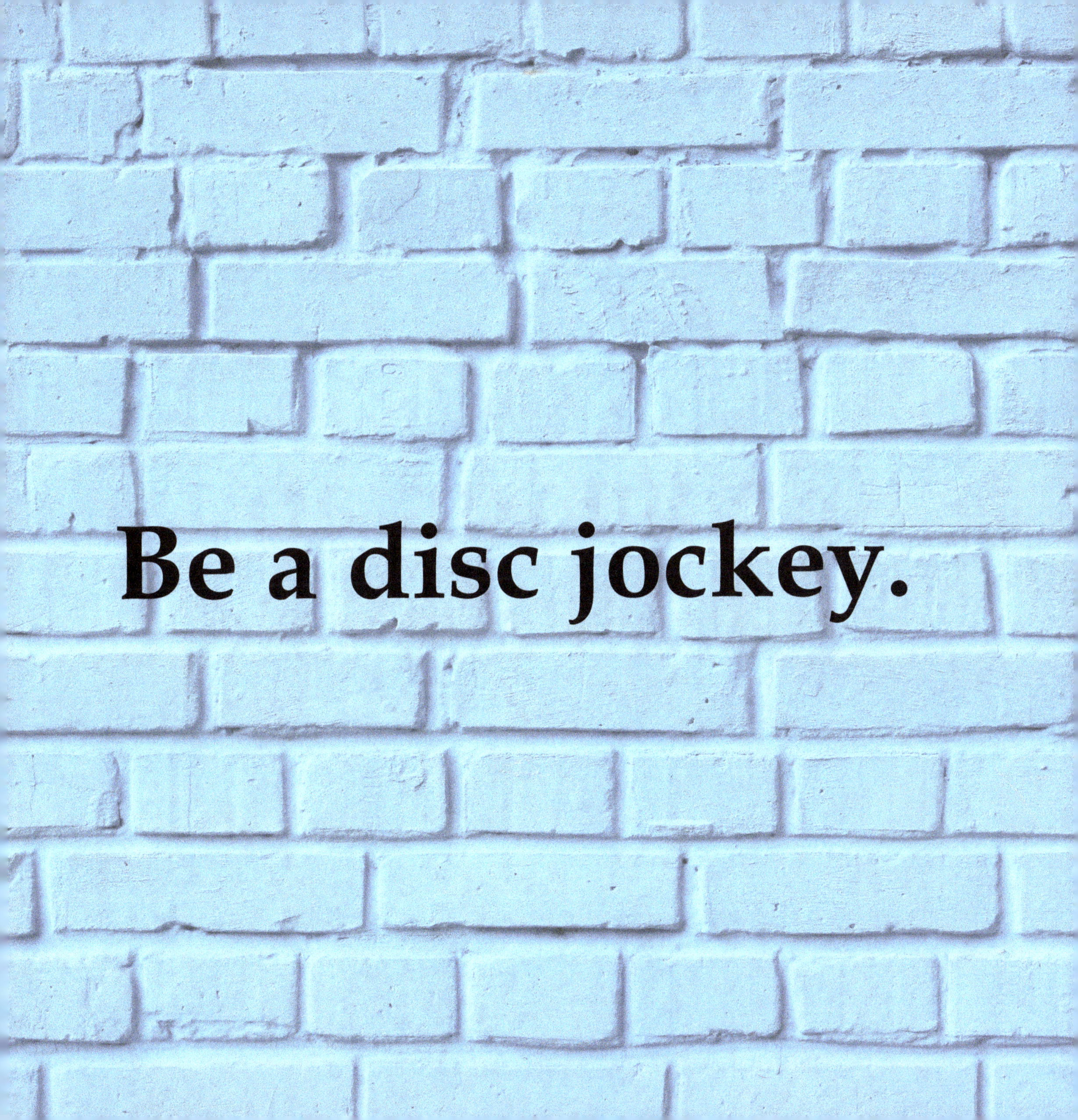
Be a disc jockey.

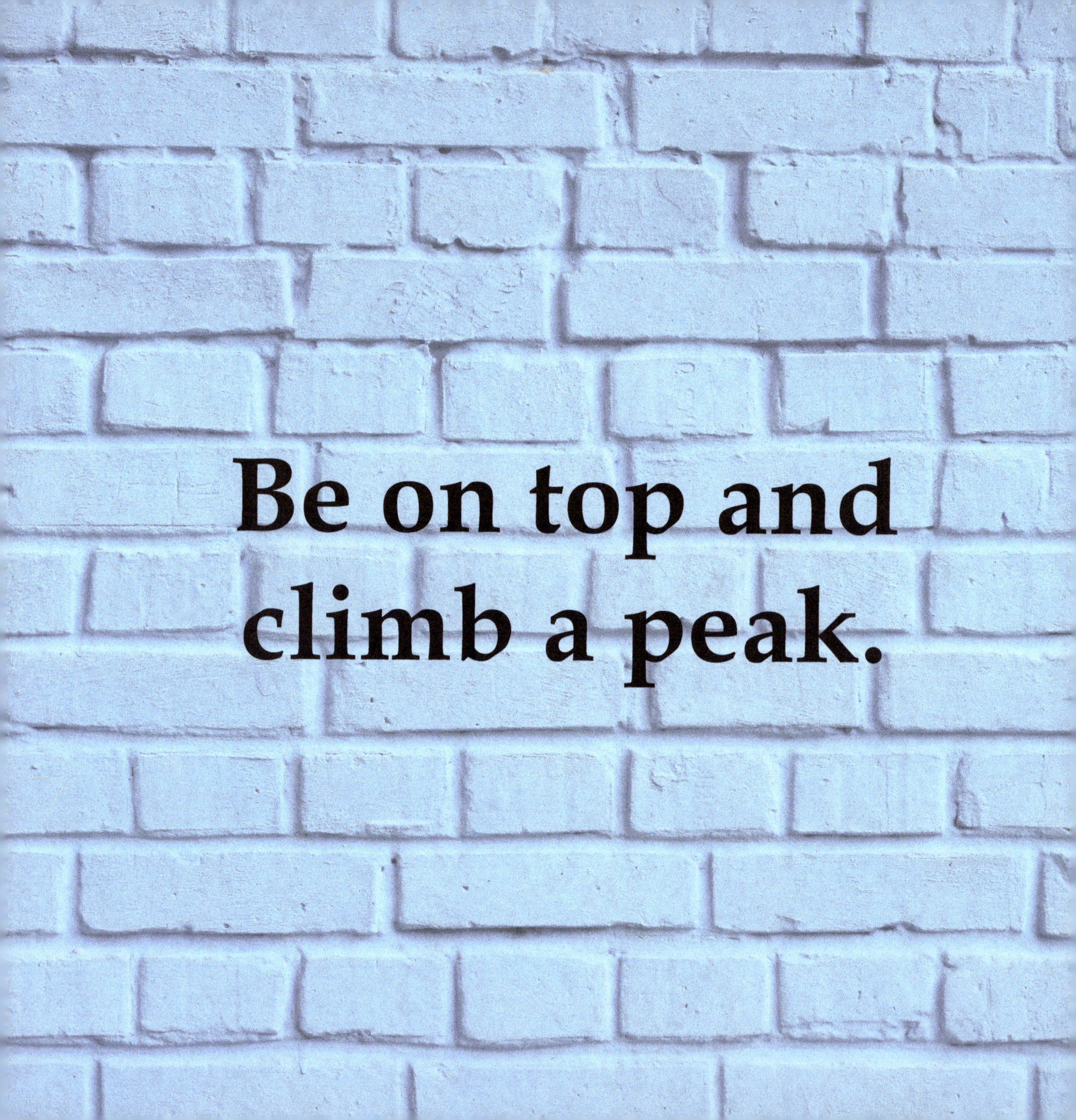
Be on top and
climb a peak.

Go to adventure parks.

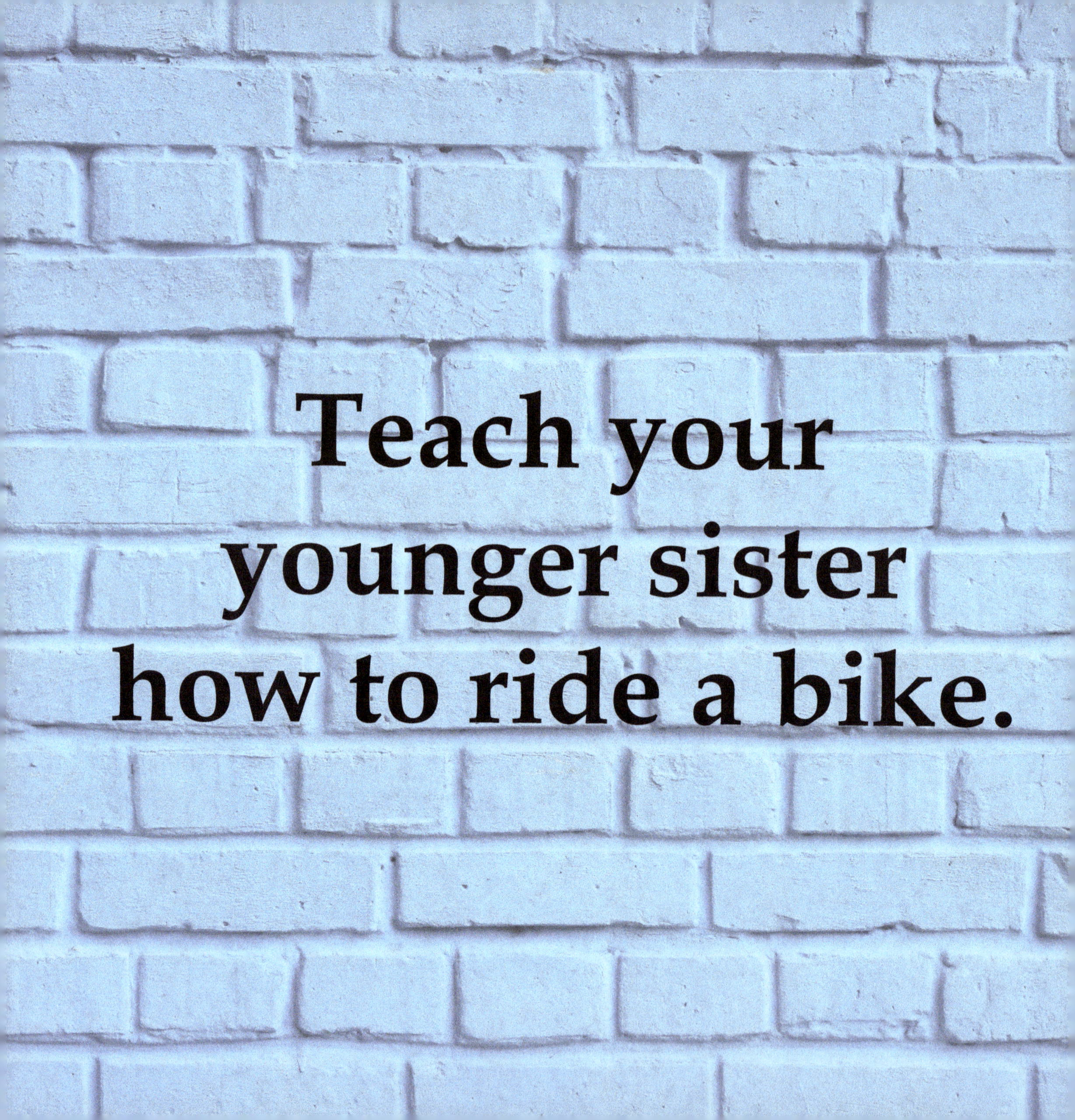

Teach your
younger sister
how to ride a bike.

Play basketball.

Try horseback
riding.

Stroll in parks
with roller
skates on.